A POCKET DICTIONARY OF
PUBL

Henry Jacob

A Pocket Dictionary of Publishing Terms

including explanations and definitions of words and phrases commonly used in the production and distribution of books

MACDONALD AND JANE'S · LONDON

ISBN 0 354 04016 2

Edited by Antony Kamm

First published 1976 by
Macdonald and Jane's Publishers Ltd.,
Paulton House,
8 Shepherdess Walk, London N1 7LW

Reproduced and printed by photolithography and
bound in Great Britain at The Pitman Press, Bath

PREFACE

This book arose out of the need to communicate with entrants to the publishing industry in Britain and overseas. The entries cover terms which publishers have made their own, often differing from or additional to their dictionary meanings, and others which publishers and others connected with the industry use or come across in their day-to-day work. Those accounting and management terms have been included which have a particular application to publishing. Terms which are completely self-explanatory or which can as readily be found in an ordinary dictionary have been omitted to retain the advantages of a pocket book; so have historical facts and contributions by individual publishers, printers and typographers. For the same reason, descriptions of a technique, process or material have deliberately been kept as short and as concise as possible; for further information the reader is advised to consult an expert in that field, or a larger reference work, such as Hugh Williamson's *Methods of Book Design*, Sean Jennett's *The Making of Books*, Judith Butcher's *Copy-editing*, etc. Equivalent terms current in the United States of America and Canada have been included where this seemed useful, for publishing is an international activity.

As techniques develop and become more sophisticated, so language develops with them. Language should be regarded as a living instrument of communication, shedding terms and adding new ones all the time, and defining, ever more precisely, connotations which, out of context, might remain incomprehensible to those outside the industry and to many within it. It is intended that new terms will be added wherever these can make a further contribution to the book's usefulness.

H.J.
January 1976

ACKNOWLEDGMENTS

I am grateful to Mr R.E. Martin and his publishers, the Book Development Council, for permission to extract terms from *A Glossary of Book Trade Terminology*, and to many others whose comments and help have made a contribution to the preparation of this book.

My thanks are especially due to Antony Kamm, who made valuable suggestions for the inclusion of new terms and definitions.

FOREWORD

by Hugh Williamson

When I was trained as a printer thirty years ago, I had to learn the terms of the trade, some derived from the long history of the printed book, others from more recent technical innovations. On entering publishing I encountered still more words and phrases new to me, defining items of publishing and business procedure and of books themselves. When in due course I came to write about the making of books, I found how difficult some of these terms were in definition, and how ambiguous they could prove in use. Students of publishing today will find they meet the same problem, and even some experience of publishing will not always resolve it. This little dictionary will be useful to publishers and aspirant publishers all over the English-speaking world.

Henry Jacob has long been interested in linguistic development, and has written a number of books and other publications, including *On Language Making* (1948) and *Printed English* (1950). I am proud to possess a copy of Beatrice Warde's *The Crystal Goblet* (1956) which he edited and she gave me. Towards the end of his long experience in publishing, Mr Jacob was in charge of the publications of the British Museum. For a number of years he and I have been concerned with lectures on the principles of publishing for developing countries, and he is now concentrating much of his time on this subject. His compilation of this book is based on extensive experience as a writer, publisher, and teacher, and the dictionary's usefulness is enhanced by its origin in this experience.

Oxford
May 1976

Items printed in *italic* are further explained under separate entries.

abridged edition shortened version of a book

accessions books added by a library to its collection

accounting terms

BALANCE SHEET annual account of the finances of a company; includes a capital account, current liabilities and provisions, fixed assets and current assets, as well as a separate trading account

INVOICE bill setting out the charges for goods or services supplied on credit

RECEIPT document acknowledging that goods or monies have been received

STATEMENT summary of charges made against a credit account, the total to be paid within a fixed period

TRADING ACCOUNT part of a *balance sheet* showing financial movement of income and expenditure over a given period, normally a year; also known as profit and loss account

advance sum paid by a publisher to an author which is set against future *royalties*; it is not returnable, even if the royalties do not reach the sum advanced·

advance copies finished copies of a new book ordered by the publisher before the delivery of the *bulk* supply; see also *reading copy*

agent (1) one who acts on behalf of an author or publisher in the negotiation and sale of *rights*, retaining for his services a percentage of monies received; (2) one who holds *stock* of the books of one or more publishers, usually overseas, for sale to booksellers in a particular country or region; see also *literary agent*, *scout*

agreement (**or contract**) document between publisher and author or editor or translator or illustrator, or between two publishers, in which the obligations of each party are defined, and the division of earnings from the sale of *rights*, e.g. paperback, film, broadcasting, translation, serial, etc., is set out

answer response, by a publisher to a bookseller, to an order for an individual book which is not available. The following abbreviations are in common use:

BDG/ND	binding, no date
NE/ND	new edition, no date
NK	not known
NYP	not yet published
OO	on order (i.e. from the printer's or binder's warehouse)
OP	out of print
RP/ND	reprinting, no date
RP/Nov	reprinting, November
RP/UC	reprint under consideration
TOP	temporarily out of print

anthology collection of the work of several authors, often of poetry, made by one or more editors or compilers

antiquarian books copies of books at least 75 years old; rare books are those which are less than 75 years old and are unobtainable from the publisher: both types may be found in antiquarian or second-hand bookshops

antique paper paper with a rough surface, good for book printing because it is light and bulky: antique paper may be *wove* or *laid*

appendix (plural **appendices**) supplementary material at the end of a book additional to the main text; see also *end-matter*

art paper paper coated with china clay used in *letterpress* and litho halftone printing (U.S. enamel); see also *paper*

artwork coloured or black and white drawings, designs or photographs arranged, *marked up*, etc., and ready for reproduction

ascender part of a letter which extends above the *x-height*, such as in b, d, f, h, l, etc.; descenders are those parts which extend below the x-height, such as in g, p, q, etc.

audio-visual aids properly educational materials which one can look at and hear simultaneously, e.g. films, sound film-strips, etc., but often used as a term to describe also materials which call on only one of these senses at a time, e.g. sound tapes, radio, slides, etc.

author's alterations (or **author's corrections**) alterations to a proof made, either by the author or the publisher, after the original *copy* has been set in type; author's alterations are charged by the printer, while typesetting errors are corrected free of charge

author's copies complimentary copies of a book, usually six, presented by a publisher to the author on publication

back margin (or **back**) margin or space on the inside of a book page near the *spine*, measured from type matter to fold; see also *gutter*

back up to print the reverse side of a sheet when the obverse has already been printed; see also *perfecting*

backlist books on a publisher's *list* published before the current season; the term is also used to refer to those books which a publisher keeps *in print* because of continuing demand

balance sheet annual account of the finances of a company, including assets and liabilities, and *profit and loss account*

basic weight the substance of a paper expressed in pounds weight for a *ream* (500 sheets) of the basic size for that particular grade; this method is becoming obsolete and is being replaced by grammes per square metre per sheet = g/m^2 or gsm

bastard title see *half-title*

battered piece of type which has become damaged and should be replaced

bed the smooth steel surface on which the type or *forme* rests in a machine which prints by *letterpress*

Bible paper thin, opaque paper made of new cotton or linen rags

bibliography (1) the science of books, their history, production, etc.; the bibliographical details of a book are found on the front and back of its title page, and include publisher's name, year of publication, printer, etc.; see *imprint*; (2) list of books on a subject or by a particular author

binder's brass *block* cut in brass or cheaper alloy for putting lettering or a design on the binding case of a book (U.S. binder's die); see also *zinco*

binder's trim the amount of paper cut from the *fore-edge*, top and *tail* of a book before it is *cased*, standardised now to 3mm or ⅛″ for work that does not *bleed*

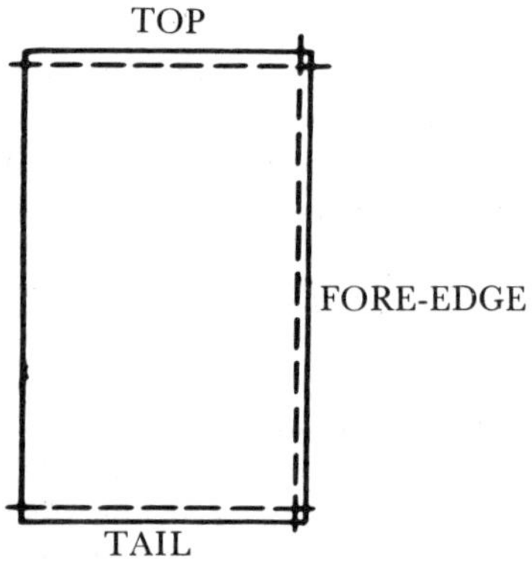

bleed (of any printed matter, but usually an illustration) to run off the edge of the page after the book is trimmed

blind blocking impression into the binding case of a book without the use of *foil* or ink; see also *binder's brass*, *blocking*, *tooling*

block any kind of engraved printing surface used in *letterpress* (U.S. cut); it is better to distinguish between a *line block*, on which the design is represented by solid lines, and a *halftone block*, on which the design is represented by dots of equal density but varying size

blocking impression of lettering or a design into the binding case of a book either using gold, silver or other coloured foil, or using ink, or *blind* (U.S. stamping); see also *binder's brass*, *tooling*, *zinco*

blurb notice written to inform the potential reader of a book; normally found on the front flap of the *jacket*, if the book has one, or else on the *half-title* and/or the back cover; also in a publisher's catalogue or advertisement

boards stiff material used to bind a book; 'boards' in the description of a book means that the book has a hard cover but no *jacket*

body (1) rectangular piece of metal which carries the letter or character for *letterpress* printing, measured in *points* from back to front; in the Anglo-American point system, 6 points = 0·083 inches; see also *type*; (2) the main text of a book as distinct from displayed or quoted matter, footnotes and captions

bold version of a type design in which each character is thickened; used for emphasis, particularly in dictionaries, directories and newspapers (U.S. bf = bold or blackface); on some machines casting solid lines of type, the *matrix* contains the *roman* as well as the **bold** or *italic* versions of a character, and thus all will be of the same width

bolts folded edges of a sheet before the book is trimmed, hence head bolt, *fore-edge* bolt, *tail* bolt; the folded edge at the back is known as the last fold or back fold

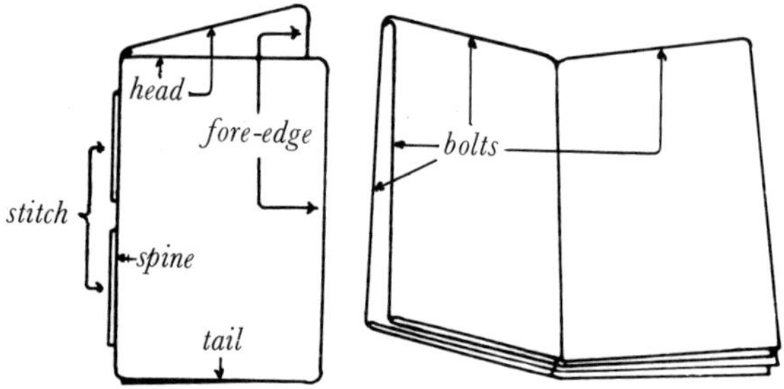

book the only known agreement as to what constitutes a book is that made at a UNESCO conference in 1950, 'a non-periodical literary publication containing forty-nine or more pages, not counting the covers'

book club organisation which sells to the public what are normally specially produced *editions* of published works, often by direct mail; members of a book club are usually required to choose in advance from a selected range of books

book sizes some untrimmed sizes are

	UK	US
Crown octavo (8vo)	7½″ x 5″ (191 x 127mm)	7½″ x 5″ (191 x 127mm)
Demy 8vo	8¾″ x 5⅝″ (222 x 143mm)	8″ x 5½″ (203 x 140mm)
Medium 8vo	9″ x 5¾″ (229 x 146mm)	9½″ x 6″ (243 x 152mm)
Royal 8vo	10″ x 6¼″ (254 x 159mm)	10″ x 6½″ (254 x 165mm)

To arrive at quarto (4to) sizes, double the measurement of the shorter side of octavo books; see also *paper sizes*

bookseller one who retails copies of books to the public or to libraries or to other institutions; see also *educational contractor*, *library supplier*, *wholesaler*

brass see *binder's brass*

break-even point point at which a publisher has sold sufficient copies of a book for the receipts from sales to balance against his direct initial investment (U.S. get-out)

broadside the unfolded sheet of any standard paper size; names such as crown, demy, medium and royal indicate the traditional size of the sheet; see also *paper sizes*

brochure (1) short work, normally *saddle-stitched* with wire; (2) lavishly produced advertising leaflet; see also *pamphlet*

bromide photographic print with glossy surface, sensitised with bromide emulsion; also known as glossy print

bulk (1) the thickness of a sheet of paper or a book without its cover; the bulk of a sheet of paper is measured with a caliper gauge; a better guide to the final look of the book is the thickness *dummy*, made up of the actual paper to be used; (2) (of delivery) the whole or main part of the total order given to a printer for finished copies of a book; see also *advance copies*

C.I.F. carriage, insurance, freight; see also *F.O.B.*

calendered paper paper smoothed under moisture, heat and pressure

camera-ready copy positive, *right-reading* matter assembled for direct reproduction for printing by *lithography* (U.S. flat); *formes*, imposed pages and complete designs can be *dry-mounted* in position on large boards for speedy and economic photography; see also *reproduction*

cancel printed leaf to be pasted into a printed book in place of a page which may have contained a serious error; a cancel title page enables a book to be sold under the *imprint* of a different publisher

capital in publishing, the amount of money needed as an investment to equip the publishing house and to finance the publication of *titles*

capitals (or **caps**) A, B, C, in contrast to a, b, c; see also *small capitals*

caption descriptive words or lines accompanying an illustration; also referred to as legend or underline

cartridge paper a strong, rough-surfaced paper used as *endpapers* for books, as drawing paper, etc.

case (1) shallow tray containing type for hand *composition* – the upper case holding capital letters, *small capitals* and figures, the lower case the rest of the characters; hence the use of 'upper case' to describe capitals, and 'lower case' to describe the small letters; (2) hard cover of a book

case-bound bound in hard cover made separately by machine or hand and usually attached to the book by means of *tapes*, gauze and *endpapers*

cash-flow balance of actual receipts against money needed for expenditure during a given period or at a particular time; an adverse balance, no matter how much money is owed by debtors, can lead to difficulty, especially in publishing in which the number of debtors in the form of booksellers with credit accounts is likely to be high

cast off character or word count of a typescript, normally made chapter by chapter, to assess its length when set in type; if one estimates that the average English word consists of six characters plus one space, the following table, using this as a unit of measurement, can serve as an approximate guide:

number of pages in book	160	192	224
number of text pages, leaving out prelims and end-matter	146	178	210
number of words or units to a printed text page			
340 words	49600	60500	71400
350 words	51100	62300	73500
420 words	61300	74700	88200
450 words	65700	80100	94500
(all figures to nearest hundred)			

number of pages in book	256	288	320
number of text pages, leaving out prelims and end-matter	238	270	294
number of words or units to a printed text page			
340 words	80900	91800	99900
350 words	83300	94500	102900
420 words	99900	113400	123500
450 words	107100	121500	132300
(all figures to nearest hundred)			

for a language whose average number of characters to a word is, for instance, 10, the table can be adapted by using the following equation $\frac{49600 \times 7}{10} = 34720$ words or units of measurement for that language

catalogue raisonné booklist in an academic work summarising the contents of books consulted and mentioning their relevance to the published work

centre to align a line or lines of type so that the middle of each corresponds with the centre of the type *measure*

centered dot (U.S.) see *decimal point*

chase metal frame in which pages of type are arranged and secured for printing by *letterpress*; the term 'in chase' or 'imposed' refers to a book ready for printing by letterpress; see also *imposition*

cheap edition re-issue of an existing book in a modified form; see also *edition*, *run-on*

chemical wood purified wood pulp from which resins and other substances have been removed, used to make woodfree paper; chemically untreated pulp is known as *mechanical* wood, and is used for making *newsprint*

chromium-faced block *stereo* or *electro* on which a film of chrome has been deposited for better wear

chromo paper paper heavily coated with china clay to obtain a smooth surface; used by blockmakers for proofing *halftones*

close up bring lines or characters closer together by removing spacing between them

cloth term loosely used for material that covers the *boards* of a binding case; it can be of three main kinds – woven; non-woven, i.e. artificial; and p.v.c., paper-based materials with an impregnated surface

club line first line of a paragraph appearing as the last line of a page

coated paper paper with a coating of clay to improve its printing surface; used for printing of *halftones* by either *letterpress* or *lithography*

co-edition arrangement between two or more publishers with different markets, or who publish in different languages, whereby they issue the same book under their respective imprints, but jointly produced to achieve maximum economy

cold type (U.S.) composition by any means which does not require hot metal; normally the term *photo-composition* is used for work done on 'Monophoto', Fotosetter, Linofilm, 'Photon' and other machines which produce *film* or *bromides* as an end product; cold composition also refers to I.B.M., Varityper-Justowriter, done on variable-spacing typewriters; see also *photographic composition*

collate check that sections or *signatures* of a book have been *gathered* in correct sequence and that no signature has been omitted

collating mark appears on the fold of a section or *signature* of a book to show at a glance that the book is complete; such marks are normally staggered so that omissions may easily be detected

collotype *planographic* printing process in which the printing medium is gelatine evenly spread over a glass or metal plate; the image is transferred to it photographically, and in drying the gelatine crinkles and forms its own natural *screen*; such plates have a limited life but give a high-quality printed result

colophon device, design or trademark serving as a house emblem

colour chart chart showing the three *process* colours in all combinations of tints, enabling any colour to be expressed as a combination of the three

colour separation photographic process whereby specific individual colours are isolated from the coloured *artwork* for three- or four-colour reproduction for subsequent printing by *letterpress* or *lithography*; an artist can prepare his *line artwork* with the different colours already separated on *overlays*

coloured top top edge of book coloured by brushing

or spraying the surface of the trimmed pages

columns (single column s/c, double column d/c) in newspaper work double column as an instruction means that matter is to be set wider, and spread over two columns; if matter is to be set in two columns in a book, e.g. footnotes, index, etc. it is best to specify 'in two columns'

combination plate (U.S.) see *line and halftone*

commission (1) percentage of the price of goods paid to the agent or salesman who effects the sale; (2) to employ an artist or author or editor or translator for a specific task

compiler person responsible for the selection of material for an *anthology*

compose assemble type by hand or machine

composing stick hand compositor's tool in which he arranges the type

composition the assembled type

composition founts sizes of type up to 14 *point* for continuous reading in a book; most books are set in 10 pt, 11 pt, 12 pt, 13 pt or 14 pt, and exceptionally in 16 pt, often with linear white space achieved by *leading* or by casting a size of type on a larger *body*, e.g. 10 pt on 12 pt

computer typesetting method of *composition* whereby copy is transferred on to a magnetic or punched tape and corrected from a *print out*; corrections are programmed on to a separate tape which can be married with the original tape; the resulting master tape can, by computer, produce *film* of the typesetting in a fraction of the time taken by more traditional methods; computer typesetting is therefore particularly applicable to long reference works which need regularly to be up-dated

condensed design of type in which the characters are narrow

consignment books are supplied 'on consignment',

usually in bulk and for export markets, on a similar understanding to *sale or return*

contact screen screen or film used in direct contact with film or photographic plate to make a *halftone block*; such screens are now replacing the conventional glass screen, and are mainly used for 85 to 133 dot work; see also *halftone*

contract see *agreement*

copy anything to be set in type; for books one normally refers to a manuscript or typescript

copy holder person who reads aloud a text that is being checked by a *proof reader*

copy preparation that part of the *sub-editing* function which is concerned with marking *copy* with instructions for the compositor (either following a designer's layout or actually acting as a designer in choosing size of type, length of line, number of lines to a page, style of heading, captions, etc.) and in making consistent all linguistic usages, spelling, hyphenation, use of dates, style of capitalisation, etc.; a further important part of copy preparation is to gather together all possible material for *preliminary pages* and *appendices* for a book (indicating 'to follow' what is not yet available), particularly so that an exact estimate of its length can be made, and to check illustrations, captions and credits against the text; see also *house style*

copyright legal protection against the use of literary or artistic property without permission, governed and regulated by national copyright laws and by two international conventions. The Berne Copyright Union was founded in 1886 and the countries belonging to it undertake to grant reciprocal protection to the works of authors and artists who are nationals of these countries. Under the Berne convention works remain in copyright for fifty years after the death of the author. The Universal Copyright Convention was established in 1952 by UNESCO to accommodate those countries which had not acceded to the Berne convention. Protection under U.C.C. depends upon the inclusion in the work of an encircled ©, the name of the holder of the copyright, and the year of first publication. Under U.C.C. works remain in copyright for 25 years following the author's death or from first publication in cases where a country's legislation applies this measure, as does the U.S.A.

copyright – compulsory licence under the terms of an agreement reached in Paris in 1971, compulsory licences can, under certain conditions including the payment of 'just compensation', be sought to publish copyright works for use in 'teaching, scholarship or research' or 'for use in connection with systematic instructional activities'. The granting of compulsory licences requires the following minimum waiting periods after first publication, (a) works of natural and physical sciences, including mathematics, and technology – three years, (b) works of fiction, poetry, drama, music and art – seven years, (c) all other works – five years. This agreement applies to members of both the Berne convention and U.C.C. and was endorsed by the U.K. in 1971.

copyright deposit supply, which is compulsory in some countries, of a copy of each publication free of charge to a central library; in U.K. the number of copies required under the copyright act, and the number of such libraries, is six

corrigenda list of corrections to a printed book the need for which has been discovered after the book has been printed; see also *erratum*

cost sheet form, used particularly in printing establishments, on which all the costs of an order, job, product or service are listed

costing (1) method by which a printer arrives at the cost of a particular job, by setting out the cost of each operation or service involved, e.g. hourly machining rates, hourly rates of manpower, materials, handling charges, *overheads*, etc.; (2) method by which a publisher arrives at the price he will have to charge for a book, taking into account both *direct* and *indirect expenditure*; see also *estimate*, *unit cost*

courtesy discount *discount* off the price of a book allowed to members of a profession or to others at the discretion of the publisher

crease emboss heavy board serving as a book cover by means of a thin rule to facilitate opening and closing and to prevent it breaking or tearing; see also *scoring*

credit (or **credit line**) acknowledgment to the artist or photographer or owner of the copyright of an illustration; appears under the illustration or in the list of illustrations or in a separate list of acknowledgments

cropping elimination of unwanted areas of an illustration, for instance by marking it on the back or on an *overlay*; see *masking*, *retouching*

cut (U.S.) see *block*

cut edges all edges of a book trimmed by guillotine

cylinder press printing machine which makes an impression on the paper by means of a cylinder rather than the flat surface of a *platen*; see also *press*

dandy roll roller on a papermaking machine which impresses wire marks on to the pulp, creating watermarks

decimal point raised dot recommended for monetary values, e.g. $10·50 (U.S. centered dot or space dot)

deckle the width of a papermaking machine

deckle edge rough natural edge on hand-made

paper; sometimes produced artificially for effect on machine-made paper

dedication inscription in a book to honour a relative or friend, usually appearing on a right-hand page immediately after the *title-page*

deep-etch to remove the background from a *halftone* block, for example, to be able to print a pencil drawing without any background dots

definitive work book which deals authoritatively with a subject and is considered at the time to be the final pronouncement on it

delivery note document to be signed by a recipient confirming delivery of goods

demy see *book sizes*, *paper sizes*

descender that part of a letter which extends below the *x-height*, as in g, p, q, etc.; see also *ascender*

design (of a book) to plan and direct its *typography*, illustration and physical production

Dewey decimal classification internationally-used system of library classification based on ten broad subject groups, each divided into ten sections, and further divided as necessary; the main groups are

000	general works
100	philosophy
200	religion
300	social sciences
400	language
500	pure science
600	applied science, technology, useful arts
700	the arts
800	literature
900	history, geography, biography

diacritical marks accents, dots and other linguistic signs above or below letters

diaeresis two dots above a vowel; in German altering the sound of the vowel, in English indicating that the vowel is pronounced separately

didot system of type measurement used on the continent of Europe

die case (or **matrix case**) mould of a *Monotype hot-metal* typecasting machine containing the *matrices* or dies of *type*

direct costs, direct expenditure cost of materials and services which can be directly attributed to a particular *title*

discount percentage reduction off the *list price* offered by a publisher to a bookseller; the amount of the discount can vary according to the number of copies ordered, the kind of order (e.g. *firm*, *sale or return*, *subscription*), and the type of book and of bookseller; see also *terms*

diss, distribute to break up *standing type* for melting down or, for hand composition, replacing it in its *case*

dot-for-dot reproduction of a coarse screen *halftone* by treating it as line artwork; usually involves some loss of quality

double sheet unfolded sheet size obtained by doubling the shorter side of a standard sheet of paper; for example, double demy; see also *paper sizes*

double-spread two facing pages; an illustration or table is referred to as double-spread when it runs across two pages

drawn-on cover style of binding in which a paper cover is glued on to a spine comprising several *signatures*; if end-papers are pasted to the cover for strength, it is known as drawn-on solid

drive-out to increase the depth of type matter on a page by adding to the material in a paragraph on the same or an earlier page or increasing its length by taking a word over to the next line; to *take back* is the opposite process and involves saving one line or more; both processes are used particularly to avoid *widows* and *club lines*

drop initial initial letter which extends over two or three lines at the beginning of a chapter, using *titling* characters; see also *titling*

dry mounting method of mounting matter for photography which ensures its perfect flatness

dry-offset *letterpress* printing process which uses three cylinders, offsetting the type image on to paper between the blanket and impression cylinders

dummy book made up of the paper and materials to be used for the finished article, but from unprinted sheets; it shows the *bulk* of the book and the thickness of the *spine*, information needed by the *jacket* designer; a dummy containing a few specimen printed *double-spreads* is also used to gain initial reactions from booksellers and foreign publishers

dust cover see *jacket*

e.g. Latin exempli gratia = for example

edit (of a book) to ensure that as far as possible, and especially by working in cooperation with the author, the original conception of the author or publisher is presented in the most suitable form; see also *sub-edit*, *editorial work*

edition (1) form in which a literary work is published, e.g. revised, original, enlarged, etc.; (2) all the copies of a book printed without alteration to text or *format*, whether or not they are printed at one time; see also *impression*, *reprint*

edition, cheap normally copies of a book printed on cheaper or smaller paper, and with a more economic form of binding, often *paper-bound*; may also be issued from the remaining sheet *stock* when the market for the original edition is satisfied; sometimes copies of the original edition sold at a reduced price; see also *remainder*

editorial work that part of the activities of a publisher which concerns the selection or commissioning of manuscripts, relations with authors and illustrators, preparing manuscripts for the printer, including checking for possible libel or for objectionable matter, checking proofs, and often, where this is not the author's responsibility, clearing of copyright for quotations and illustrations; see also *copy preparation*, *proof reading*, *sub-edit*

educational contractor one who receives a contract from an educational institution or other authority to supply books and other educational materials

electro (**electrotype**) duplicate of a *halftone block* made by depositing copper on a mould; the resulting copper skin is backed with lead and mounted, and is then ready for *letterpress* printing

elision omission of inessential matter, e.g. rendering 1976-1977 as 1976-77

em (1) as a measurement, equal to the *point* size of the type being used, e.g. 8pt em, 10pt em; (2) as a general unit of length signifies the pica em or *pica*, 12 points wide, which is approximately 1/6 inch

em rule dash implying dissociation, often used in place of parentheses (brackets); indicated on copy by $\frac{1}{M}$

en half the *em* in any size of type; considered to be the average width of the type characters in a *fount*, and is thus useful for making approximate calculations

en rule dash implying association, e.g. 1850-80; indicated on copy by $\frac{1}{N}$

end-matter pages at the end of a book containing matter which is not part of the main text, e.g. *appendices*, *bibliography*, *index*, etc. (U.S. back matter)

endpapers four pages attached to the beginning of the first section of a book, and four to the end of the last section, the outer page in each case being pasted on to the cover; normally made of plain white *cartridge* paper, though printed or coloured endpapers can be used for special books (U.S. endsheets); see also *self-ends*

erratum, errata list of corrections too late to be incorporated in the printed text; may be printed at the end of the *preliminary pages*, which in a scholarly work are usually printed last, or on a slip of paper, pasted or inserted in the book; see also *corrigenda*

esparto paper fine grade of paper made of esparto grass, usually with the addition of chemical wood pulp; its advantages are strength, opacity, smoothness, high bulk

estimate (1) price quoted by a printer for a particular job according to the publisher's specification; (2) detailed listing by a publisher of all *direct expenditure* which will be incurred in producing a particular book; also called house estimate; see also *costing*, *unit cost*

etch to engrave a design on a printing plate by means of acid

even small caps capital characters which align with the *x-height* of their *fount*, A, B, C, etc., and which do not have *capitals* at the beginning of a word or name

even working book that can be completed in sections of 16, 32, 48, or 64 pages, and not requiring an additional oddment of 4 or 8 pages

F.O.B. (carriage term) free on board; see also *C.I.F.*

f.s.e. folded, sewn and *endpapered* copies of books, stored or supplied ready for immediate placing in the binding cases

facsimile reproduction of an original, true in every respect, with no reduction or enlargement

fair dealing right which allows the copying of even a substantial part of a copyright work for the purpose of research, private study, published criticism or a *review*

fee sum of money paid outright for particular services; sometimes to an author on delivery of manuscript in place of a *royalty*, but more usually to an illustrator, translator, contributor of a *foreword*, etc.

film photographic film in positive or negative form from which *plates* can be made for printing by *lithography*

filmsetting photosetting technique which produces film as an end-product, also referred to as *photocomposition*

finishing all the book production processes after the sheets of a book have been printed

firm books supplied to a bookseller and invoiced on agreed terms for payment within a given time

flap that part of the *jacket* of a book which is folded round the inside of the binding case, often carrying a description of the book, its price, and other announcements; see also *blurb*

flat-bed letterpress machine that prints from a flat *forme*; see also *press*

flat sheets printed, unfolded sheets of a book

foil thin leaf of metal on a paper base used for *blocking* the binding case of books

folded and collated (f. and c.) folded, *gathered* and *collated* unbound sheets of a book, often the form in which *stock* is held for later binding; an economic method of storage since *overs* of any one or more sheets can then be destroyed

foliation consecutive numbering of *double-spreads*, particularly in manuscript books, reference being made to *verso* and *recto* (i.e. 10v and 10r), as distinct from numbering each page *(pagination)*

folio (1) printed page number; (2) size obtained by folding a standard sheet (i.e. *broadside*) of paper in half, thus making four pages

footnote note at the foot of a page normally set 2pt smaller than the size of the text. In scholarly works, where such notes abound, they may be numbered with *superior figures* either page by page or chapter by chapter; though, as an economy measure, such notes are often collected at the end of each chapter, or all together as part of the *end-matter*

fore-edge the outer edge of a page or book opposite to the spine

foreword introductory note, often by an authority on the subject, explaining the value of a book; see also *introduction*, *preface*, *preliminary pages*

format inclusive term for the size, shape and general layout of a book; two basic formats are

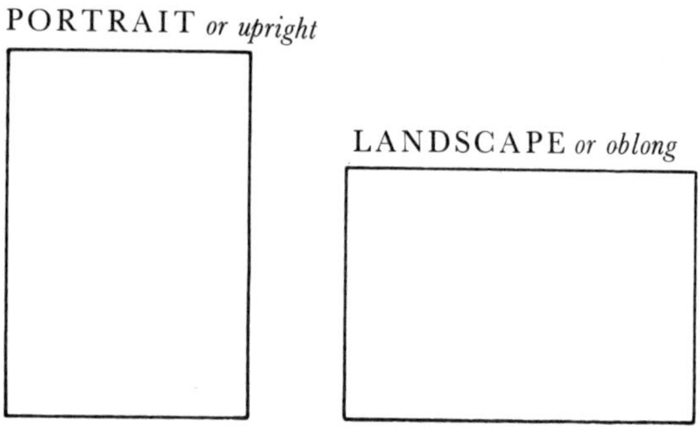

forme *chase* and its contents ready for printing by *letterpress*; also complete *film* or *camera-ready copy* for printing by *lithography*

forwarding all the operations in binding a book from folding the sheets up to but not including putting on the cover or binding case; see also *finishing*

fount complete set of type of a given design and size; the same design of type in a variety of sizes is known as a family

four line mathematics system for the composition of complex mathematical equations

french fold sheet of paper printed on one side only

and folded with *bolts* left uncut; used for invitations, etc.

front-matter see *preliminary pages*

frontispiece illustration facing a title page

fugitive description of colours or inks which fade when exposed to light; opposite of *light-fast*

full binding (**full bound**) hard binding whose covering material extends over the whole area of *spine* and *boards*; see also *half-binding* and *quarter-binding*

full out instruction to begin type matter without any *indentation*

full point full stop

furniture non-printing material for filling out space in a *chase* after the type has been put into it

galley flat, oblong tray which holds metal type; galley proofs are the first *proofs* taken after the text has been *composed* and before it is divided into pages; see also *page-proof*

gather to assemble sections or *signatures* of a book; see also *collate*

general reserve financial term used to describe a safeguard against possible future losses over a general area of current assets, e.g. bad debt reserve of 5% over total outstanding debtors

glassine see *lamination*

gold used for lettering on book bindings and for tops; if supplied in leaf form or as leaves placed on thin backing material it is known as *foil*; most bindings are stamped in imitation gold

grain (or **machine direction**) direction in which paper forms itself on a paper-making machine; normally in printing the grain should run parallel to the spine of the book for easy opening and the avoidance of buckling; however for lithographic colour printing, paper with the grain running at right angles to the spine of the book is usually chosen; this avoids stretch with consequent loss of *register* due to the presence of water absorbed by the paper on the printing machine

grammage substance of paper expressed in grammes per square metre per sheet = g/m^2 or gsm

gravure (**photogravure**) high-speed *intaglio* printing process in which the image is engraved on a copper cylinder for printing in one or more colours; mainly used for printing magazines with large editions; see also *printing processes*

grippers mechanical fingers, used in *sheet-fed* printing to hold the sheet of paper in the correct position on the machine; when the design of a book is being planned, allowance must be made for the edge of the grippers in placing illustrations; if illustrations are to *bleed* it may be necessary to print on a sheet larger than would otherwise be required

gross profit profit figure on a publisher's balance sheet which shows *direct expenditure* balanced against receipts; *overheads*, for instance, are not taken into account when arriving at this figure

grotesque (**'grot'**) the name of a much-used *sans-serif typeface*, but, loosely, any sans-serif typeface

guarding strips of paper or linen sewn in with the *signatures* of a book, to which individual illustration *plates* or sections of plates are pasted

gutter (1) space between the *fore-edges* of pages where they fall internally in the imposed *forme*; (2) loosely used for the space made by the *back margins* of two facing pages

half-binding hard binding case of which the spine and corners are covered with one material, the rest with another, usually paper; see also *full binding* and *quarter binding*

half-title right-hand page immediately preceding the title page, usually carrying the title of the book only; sometimes called bastard title; see also *part-title*

halftone reproduction which conveys the varying tonal values of a continuous tone photograph, illustration or design; the original is photographed through a screen which divides up the image into dots of equal density but varying size, thus giving the impression of shading and tones; also loosely applied to originals for reproduction as halftones; see also *block*, *photo-engraving*

halftone block relief engraving for printing a *halftone* by *letterpress*; see also *line block*

half-up description of an illustration which has been drawn 1½ times the size it will appear in the finished book; also referred to as 3:2

hanging indent(**ation**) first line of text *full out*, subsequent lines indented

head margin white space at the top of a page

headband coloured silken cord glued to the *spine* to ornament the top edge of a *cased* book

heading displayed line of type naming the title of a chapter or part or paragraph

headline see *running head*

height-to-paper see *type-height*

heliogravure form of printing from copper plates; loosely used to describe *gravure*

hot-metal *composition* by means of a machine which casts single characters or complete lines in hot metal; see also *cold type*, *photographic composition*

hourly rate cost to a printer of running a particular machine for one hour; in the same way manpower is costed on an hourly rate basis

house style system of rules followed by publisher or printer (the latter if not otherwise instructed) to ensure consistency of spelling and linguistic usage

I.B.M. (composition) proprietary method of composing *justified* or *unjustified* type by means of a carbon film ribbon on an electric composing machine for use as an original for reproduction for printing by lithography

i.e. Latin id est = that is

I.S.B.N. (International Standard Book Number) ten-digit number allocated to each separate publication, including each new *edition* of a work; it is divided into four parts – the first part is the group identifier (i.e. a country or group of countries), the second the publisher identifier, the third the title identifier, the fourth a check digit; a computer will first check that a number fed into it is a valid one, the numbers being multiplied successively by 10, 9, 8, 7, 6, 5, 4, 3 and 2, which are called weights; the products are then added together and divided by the modulus 11; if there is no remainder, the number is valid; for example

	group identifier	publisher prefix				title number				check digit
I.S.B.N.	0	8	4	3	6	1	0	7	2	7
weight	10	9	8	7	6	5	4	3	2	
products	0	72+32+21+36				+5+0+21+4				+7

total 198 which, divided by modulus 11, produces a valid I.S.B.N.; see also *Library of Congress Catalog Card Number*

ibidem, ibid. Latin = to be found in the same place

idem, id. Latin = the same (i.e. in the same title)

imitation art paper with a high filler content and heavily *calendered* to achieve a smooth surface akin to art paper

imposition arrangement of pages of type matter in correct position for folding when printed; the imposition varies according to the folding machine to be used

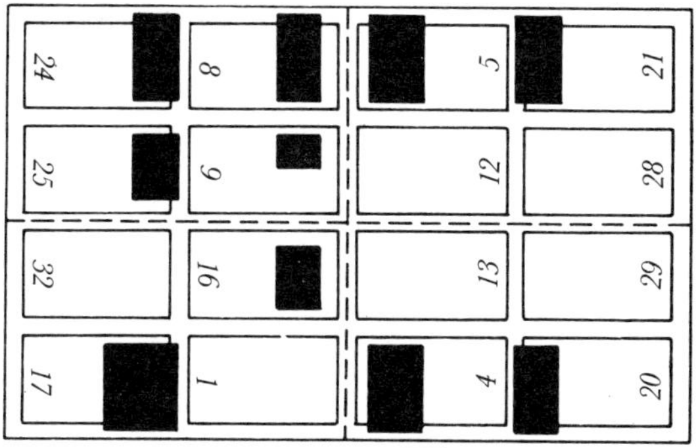

--- *chase bars* ■ *block area*

impression all the copies of a book printed at one time from the same type or plates; see also *edition*, *reprint*

imprimatur Latin = let it be published; licence still needed in some secular and religious communities stating 'nihil obstat' (nothing hinders), and dated and signed; to publish a work 'under the imprimatur of . . .' means that it is sponsored in some way by that organisation

imprint (1) name of a book's publisher appearing at the bottom of the title page; (2) information, normally printed on the reverse of the title page, about the book's copyright, publisher, printer, etc.; see also *bibliography*

imprint page reverse of the title page

in print *title* or titles of which the publisher holds *stock*

inches to centimetres, conversion

inch	cm
½	1·27
1	2·54
2	5·08
3	7·62
4	10·16
5	12·70
6	15·24
7	17·78
8	20·32
9	22·86
10	25·40
20	50·80
30	76·20
40	101·60

incunabulum (plural **incunabula**) book or books printed from movable type before A.D. 1500; those printed from wood engraved blocks are called block books

indent (1) to buy on open or credit account; (2) instruction to typesetter to arrange white space at beginning of line or paragraph

indent(**ation**) white space appearing at the beginning of a line; the indent at the beginning of a paragraph is usually one *em* of the type size

index alphabetical list of names and/or topics mentioned in a book, with page references; the list can be divided into author, subject, geographical index, etc.

Index Translationum *bibliography* of translations published annually by UNESCO since 1949; from 1932 to 1940 it was published by League of Nations

indirect cost expenditure on services which cannot be attributed to a particular book, e.g. *overheads*; see also *direct cost*

inferior figures see *superior figures*

in-house work work which a publisher can have done without recourse to outside services, e.g. diagrams drawn by his design department

insert section of at least four pages so placed that in a 16-page *signature* the first two pages will come between the fourth and fifth pages of the signature, and the last two between the twelfth and thirteenth pages; see also *inset*, *tip-in*, *wrap*

inset section of at least four pages placed in the middle of a signature; see also *insert*, *tip-in*, *wrap*

inspection copy copy of a book, usually a classroom textbook, offered by the publisher to a teacher to examine for an agreed time, at the end of which the book must be returned or paid for; however, often the copy may be retained free of charge if a requisite number of further copies are bought

intaglio printing processes in which the ink lies in incisions on the surface of a metal plate, their depth governing the density of the resulting image, e.g. *gravure* (either on a *flat-bed* or *rotary* machine); see also *printing processes*

interleave introduce blank pages alternate to the printed text on which additions, corrections, notes, etc. can be made (U.S. slip-sheeting)

introduction preliminary matter to the text of a book, either by the author or by an authority on the subject, and coming immediately before it; usually longer and less personal than a *preface* or *foreword*; see also *preliminary pages*

italic type which slopes to the right, mainly used for emphasis, and originally deriving from handwritten characters

jacket (also **dustcover**, **wrapper**) printed paper covering placed round a *case-bound* book originally to protect the binding but now used to attract sales; the *blurb* usually appears on the front *flap*

jobber (U.S.) person or organisation holding books from different publishers for sale to retail booksellers and libraries

jobbing printer printer who deals mainly in wide variety of small printing requirements, e.g. letter headings, business cards, stationery, stickers, labels, etc., not bookwork

jobbing types types used for ephemeral printing and not normally suitable for book printing

journey terms special *discounts* for books from a publisher's *backlist* on orders given by a bookseller on the occasion of a visit by that *publisher's representative*

justify to space out the words in a line to a given *measure*; such lines *range* at both ends; lines whose right-hand ends are ragged are *unjustified*

keep standing retain at the printer, to whom rent is payable, the type or plates from which a book has been printed for a possible reprint; such materials should not normally be *distributed* or destroyed without the publisher being informed

laid paper *antique* paper which shows thin wire-made watermarks, or laid lines, and cross-chain marks; these marks are made on the machine by the *dandy roll* touching the damp pulp; laid marks occur naturally only in hand-made papers; see also *wove*

lamination thin transparent plastic covering impressed under heat on to a book *jacket* or cover after it has been printed, to protect it and improve its appearance (U.S. glassine); see also *varnish*

landscape description of a book whose width exceeds its depth, the opposite being *portrait*; see also *format*

lay edge edge of a sheet which on the printing machine contacts the lay gauges, whose purpose is to ensure that the printing appears in the same position on every sheet; the front edge is the gripper edge, one side edge the side lay; when *perfecting* the sheet the same edge should be used in both printings to ensure good *register*; see also *grippers*

layout design showing the arrangement of type and illustration on a page

leading additional interlinear space, so called because originally strips of lead were placed between the lines of type; spacing material from six *points* thick up is called reglets if in wood or clumps if in metal

ledger accounting control for a particular area of finance, often divided into

REAL LEDGER sales, purchases, individual accounts listed in the name of a person or company

NOMINAL LEDGER overheads, production, individual accounts listed according to type of expense or title of book or project

PRIVATE LEDGER assets and liabilities

legal deposit see copyright deposit

legend see *caption*

letter spacing additional spacing placed between letters of words set in *capitals* or *small capitals* to obtain equal optical spacing

letterpress method of printing from raised type or *blocks* in which the projecting part of the type or blocks carries the ink and presses the image on to the paper; see also *lithography*, *offset lithography*, *gravure*, *printing processes*

libel publication of defamatory matter; under English law an action for libel may involve the printer as well as publisher and author

library binding reinforced hardcover binding particularly suitable for books receiving constant use

Library of Congress Catalog Card Number number, a combination of shelf mark and *Dewey decimal classification* number, allocated to each book published in the U.S.A.; a card catalogue is issued which may be bought on subscription; the number is also printed in the book itself

library supplier one who specialises in the supply and servicing of books for libraries; see also *library binding*

light-fast inks which do not fade when exposed to light; the opposite is *fugitive*

limited edition *edition* limited to a specific number of copies, sometimes individually numbered and signed by the author

limp any form of binding in which *boards* are not used, but more usually of books whose covers are made of non-woven *cloth* than of those which are *paperbacks* or *paper-bound*

line and (half)tone *letterpress blocks* or *lithographic plates* which contain both *line* and *halftone* work, each kind being printed down from a separate piece of *film* and then *etched* in a single operation (U.S. combination plate)

line artwork illustrations, diagrams and other designs which contain no gradation of tone

line block relief engraving prepared from *line artwork* for printing by *letterpress*; see also *halftone block*

lining figures 1 2 3 4 5 6 7 8 9 0 are used for preference in tables but should be so marked by the publisher on the *copy*, though with certain type faces such as Aldine, Bembo, Caslon, etc, old face figures 1 2 3 4 5 6 7 8 9 0 (called non-lining) are normally used

Linotype literally line-of-type, a proprietary composing machine producing solid *slugs* of type, a line at a time, and similar in construction to that which is known as Intertype; a Ludlow produces small and very large characters as solid lines but *matrices* have to be hand set, whereas Linotype and Intertype use keyboards at speed; see also *Monotype*

list (1) publisher's catalogue; (2) all the books a publisher has available for sale, the terms 'spring list' or 'autumn list' referring to new books which he will publish at that time of year; see also *backlist*

list price price fixed by the publisher, which may be *net* or *non net* for a particular book, and advertised in his catalogue

literal mistake in *composition* usually made by 'tapping' the wrong character on the keyboard of the machine (U.S. typo)

literary agent one who negotiates on behalf of author or publisher the sale of *rights* in literary works, including plays, films, and television and radio programmes, receiving for his services a percentage of any monies earned

lithography *planographic* printing process much used for books, and especially for colour work, based on the fact that oil-based inks and water do not mix; direct lithography from a stone is rarely employed now; an electric typewriter can produce a perfectly satisfactory image from which printing plates can be made, and plates for *reprints* can economically be made by photographing a copy of the original book; after a certain point in the *print run* the process is cheaper than *letterpress* because the machines print at far greater speed than letterpress machines; see also *offset lithography, printing processes*

long page page in which the type matter extends below the specified type area, sometimes deliberately planned to bring the book to an *even working*

lower case (l.c.) small characters of an alphabet (a, b, c, d, e, f, etc.) as distinct from *capitals* (A, B, C, D, E, F, etc.) or *small capitals* (A, B, C, D, E, F, etc.); see also *case*

machine direction see *grain*

machine proof *proof* taken on the actual printing

machine from the *imposed* pages, usually to check the *register* and the tonal value of colour work

machining the process of printing on machine; also known as printing-off

make ready to prepare the forme and printing machine to achieve a sharp, clean and even impression or image all over the sheet, a process which takes longer for *letterpress* than for *offset*

make-up the process of dividing the *composition* into pages, and adding page numbers, *running heads*, *display lines*, etc., after corrections have been made to the *galley* proof; however where economies must be exercised books whose setting is straightforward may be put straight into page form

making order for paper which cannot be supplied from *stock*, e.g. due to a special quantity or non-standard size of sheet being required, and which has to be specially made by the paper-mill

marked proof proof with corrections and queries for the publisher by the printer's reader, usually marked in green ink

mark-up (1) increase over the *list price* of a book, normally applied in export markets where allowance has to be made for additional *overheads* when converting the price to local currency; (2) process of entering *typographical* instructions to the printer and his *compositor* on a manuscript or piece of *copy*; see also *scale*

masking (1) process used for making corrections to negatives in colour separation; (2) placing a covering over artwork to delete a portion of it

matrix (plural **matrices**) (1) mould used for casting type, e.g. at a type founder or in a matrix case for *Monotype composition* or on a *slug*-casting machine; (2) mould of a page of type or of type for an advertisement from which a *stereo* can be made

matrix case see *die case*

maximum measure maximum line width which should not be exceeded in type setting that is *unjustified*

measure specified width of line, measure in pica *ems* of which six make 72 *points* = approximately one inch

mechanical tint simulation of tonal variation which can be stuck down on an illustration or design and reproduced as *line artwork*

mechanical wood pulp or paper made from coarse chemically untreated wood-fibre; available as *newsprint* or antique mechanical; see also *chemical wood*

metric system (**système international d'unités**) **1960** recognised prefixes used are
mega- = million times
kilo- = thousand times
hecto- = hundred times
deca- = ten times
deci- = tenth part
centi- = hundredth part
milli- = thousandth part
micro- = millionth part
see also *inches to centimetres*

MF machine-finished paper with a matt surface; see also *calendered paper*

MG machine-glazed paper; see also *calendered paper*

micro- used in its non-scientific meaning to indicate a considerable photographic reduction of the size of the original, as in microfilm, microfiche, microform, microprint, etc.

mill board heavy *board* made from waste paper, mechanical pulp and sometimes of other fibres, but not straw; see also *straw-board*

mint (**condition**) description of an entirely undamaged book or books which have been offered for sale

monograph volume dealing in a scholarly way with a single subject

Monotype proprietary name of a composing machine producing single characters in hot metal by means of keyboard and caster; the same company manufactures the Monophoto for *photographic composition*; see also *Linotype*

montage combination of several drawings or photographs, or parts of them, to make up a composite design

mould (1)(in type casting) box containing a *matrix*; (2) plastic impression taken from a letterpress block in making an *electrotype*

mounted block *line* or *half tone* engraving fixed to a *type-height* base of metal and/or wood for printing by *letterpress*; type-height is 0·918 inches (23·317mm)

negative photographic image on film or glass in which the lines and tones of the original are reversed from black to white; the image can then be transferred to a metal plate; see also *positive*

net not liable to *discount* or reduction; a net book is one subject in U.K. to the Net Book Agreement which stipulates that a book must not be sold to the public at less than the *list price*; see also *non net*

net receipts sums received by a publisher in respect of the sale of books or *rights* from which commissions or discounts have been deducted

newsprint cheapest kind of book paper, made from *mechanical wood*

non net subject to discount or reduction; a non net book may be sold to the public at a *discount* off the list price; the decision as to whether a book will be *net* or non net rests with the publisher; in U.K. school textbooks are usually non net

octavo (**8vo**) size obtained by folding a sheet of paper three times, making a section of 16 pages; see also *folio*, *quarto*

offcut piece cut off a sheet of paper to reduce it to the correct size, which may still be useful for ephemeral printing

off-print separate printing or a *run-on* usually of an article in an academic journal, a number of which copies may be given to the author in place of payment (U.S. separate)

offset loosely used with the meaning to print by *lithography* from existing printed matter

offset lithography printing process in which the image is inked on the printing surface, lifted by a roller (i.e. offset on to it) and then transferred on to the paper; its characteristic is softness of impression and its ability is to print *halftones* on uncoated paper; see also *printing processes*

offset paper paper treated to resist the moisture present in lithographic printing

old style figures see *lining figures*

one-shot rights single issue *volume rights* whereby the whole of a literary work or a shortened version of it appears in a journal

opacity quality of non-transparency in paper; adjective opaque

open market territory or territories agreed between two publishers of the same book in the same language in which both parties have the right to sell their edition

opere citato, op. cit. Latin = in the work quoted

option clause statement in an *agreement*, usually between a publisher and author, that the author shall first offer his next work or works of a similar nature to that publisher

origination conversion of text matter and/or illustrations into a form from which printing *plates* can then be made; see also *camera-ready copy*

out-of-print *title* or titles of which no further copies are available from the publisher and a *reprint* is not at present contemplated; see also *answer*, *in print*

outright sale of copyright grant to a publisher, usually by an author, of all *rights* in his work in return for a cash payment instead of his being paid on a *royalty* basis

out-turn sheet specimen sheet of paper to be used for printing a particular book, sent to the publisher for his final check

outwork (1) services rendered to a printer which he cannot undertake for himself, e.g. special typesetting, binding , etc.; (2) freelance editorial or design work etc. commissioned by a publisher outside the publishing house

overheads that part of the expenditure of a publisher which cannot be attributed to a specific title except as a percentage of a year's trading, e.g. salaries, rent, general administration and accounting, distribution, etc.

overlay (1) transparent covering over a piece of *artwork* on which instructions can be marked, e.g. *scaling*, *cropping*, etc.; (2) transparent sheet on which an artist can make his own colour *separations*, each colour being drawn in black for photography either as one of the three primary colours and black, or as other colours according to a separate colour guide

overmatter composed text which exceeds the space it is meant to fill and needs editorial attention; particularly common in newspaper and periodical publishing at the stage when *galley proofs* are being pasted up as a guide to the printer for make-up; the proof of the overmatter should be returned to the printer for identification and charging purposes

overprint to print text or an inscription on matter that has already been printed, e.g. a bookseller's name on a booklist

overrun deletions or additions within a paragraph may involve resetting of several lines, which are lightly marked by the compositor as overrun and thus requiring further *proof reading*

overs sheets supplied in excess of the required number to allow for spoilage in printing and binding; different percentages are agreed between publisher and printer for colour work as opposed to work in black and white

overstocks books at bookseller or publisher for which there is little or no demand; see also *remainder*

Ozalid proprietary term for photographic proof which can be made from *imposed film* before platemaking; sometimes also referred to as 'blues' or 'Van Dykes'

page-proof *proof* of a book made up into pages; if the book has gone through the *make-up* stage but has not yet been imposed for letterpress printing, a proof can be submitted as page-on-galley, i.e. two or more pages on *galley* proof, or as slip-pages, i.e. one page on each separate slip of paper

pages-to-view pages printed on one side of a sheet; see also *imposition*

pagination numbers used to identify individual pages; especially in larger works *preliminary pages* are often numbered in roman numerals, the text matter with arabic numerals; see also *foliation*, *folio*

pamphlet normally a piece of polemical writing for mass circulation rarely exceeding 32 or 48 pages; see also *brochure*

paper product of cellulose fibres from rags, grass, wood, straw, bark and other materials mixed with chemicals, sizing, and filling and loading agents; see also *art*, *antique*, *cartridge*, *laid*, *wove*, *calendered*, *making*

paper sizes traditional sizes of paper are still being used for book production in many countries; U.K. traditional and adapted standards are given below, as well as U.S. traditional standards; for stationery, international standard paper sizes are used for economy, based on the metric system. The use of standard sizes has implications for the choice of printing machine size and the use of standardised equipment, e.g. *chases*, *furniture*, etc.; as well as reducing the cost of investment capital if planning is done in advance for all purposes and printing processes available

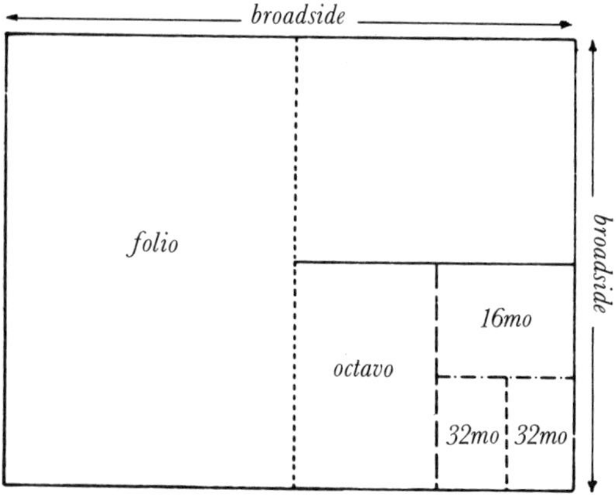

(1) CONVERSION TABLE, INCHES TO MILLIMETRES

1″	=	25·40mm
2″	=	50·80mm
4″	=	101·600mm
10″	=	254·00mm
15″	=	381·00mm
20″	=	508·00mm
30″	=	762·00mm
40″	=	1016·00mm

(2) UK TRADITIONAL UNTRIMMED PAPER SIZES FOR BOOK PRINTING

name	broadside
crown	15″ x 20 ″= 381 x 508mm
demy	17½″ x 22½ ″= 445 x 572mm
medium	18″ x 23 ″= 457 x 584mm
royal	20″ x 25 ″= 508 x 635mm

name	4to
crown	7½″ x 10 ″= 191 x 254mm
demy	8¾″ x 11¼ ″= 222 x 286mm
medium	9″ x 11½ ″= 229 x 292mm
royal	10″ x 12½ ″= 254 x 318mm

name	8vo
crown	5″ x 7½ ″= 127 x 191mm
demy	5⅝″ x 8¾ ″= 143 x 222mm
medium	5¾″ x 9 ″= 146 x. 229mm
royal	6¼″ x 10 ″= 159 x 254mm

(3) US TRADITIONAL PAPER SIZES FOR BOOK PRINTING

22″ x 32″	33″ x 44″
24″ x 36″	33″ x 46″
25″ x 39″	34″ x 44″
26″ x 39″	35″ x 45″
26″ x 40″	36″ x 48″
28″ x 42″	38″ x 50″
28″ x 44″	41″ x 51″
29″ x 52″	42″ x 56″
30½″ x 41″	44″ x 56″
32″ x 44″	44″ x 64″

(4) UK METRIC STANDARD SIZES FOR BOOK PRINTING (in mm)

	quad	4to	8vo
metric crown	768 x 1008	252 x 192	192 x 126
metric large crown	816 x 1056	264 x 204	204 x 132
metric demy	888 x 1128	282 x 222	222 x 141
metric royal	960 x 1272	318 x 240	240 x 159

binder's trim for head, *tail* and *foredge* has been standardised at 3mm for each trim for work that does not *bleed*

(5) INTERNATIONAL STANDARD PAPER SIZES (I.S.O.)

A SERIES TRIMMED

A0	841 x 1189mm	33·11″ x 46·81″
A1	549 x 841mm	23·29″ x 33·11″
A2	420 x 594mm	16·54″ x 23·29″
A3	297 x 420mm	11·69″ x 16·54″
A4	210 x 297mm	8·27″ x 11·69″
A5	148 x 210mm	5·83″ x 8·27″
A6	105 x 148mm	4·13″ x 5·83″
A7	74 x 105mm	2·91″ x 4·13″

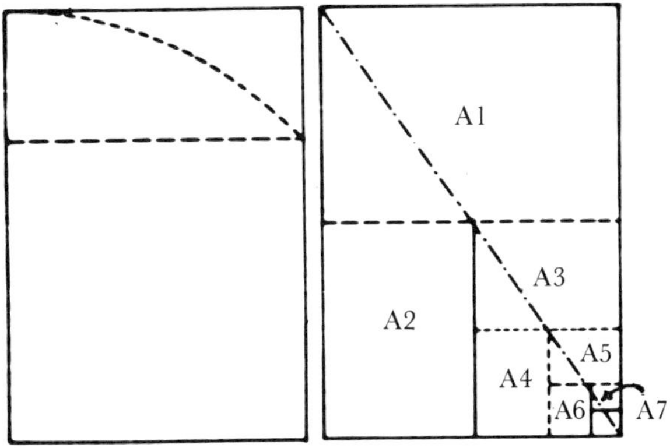

B SERIES TRIMMED

basic I.S.O. sheet based on a square metre is B0 1000 x 1414mm = 39·37″ x 55·67″

C SERIES

basic sheet of 917 x 1297mm = 36″ x 51·20″ for envelope making and similar purposes

---

paper substance conversion

gsm	demy lb/ream	medium lb/ream	royal lb/ream	crown lb/ream
20	5·60	5.89	7·11	8·53
25	7·00	7·36	8·88	10·67
40	11·20	11·78	14·22	17·07
45	12·60	13·25	16·00	19·20
50	14·00	14·72	17·78	21·34
56	15·68	16·49	19·91	23·90
63	17·64	18·55	22·40	26·88
71	19·88	20·90	25·25	30·30
80	22·40	23·55	28·45	34·14
90	25·20	26·50	32·00	38·40
100	28·00	29·44	35·56	42·67

paperback loosely any book in a soft or stiff paper cover; more specifically = U.S. pocketbook, i.e. book, normally *perfect* bound, distributed by mass market sales methods

paper-bound, **paper-covered** any book in a soft or stiff paper cover; see also *limp*, *self-cover*

part-title right-hand page carrying the title of a part of the book, the reverse being blank; see also *half-title*

pass for press to give the instruction for *machining* to proceed, subject to any marked corrections being made beforehand; the marked *proof* should be dated and retained by the printer in case of any dispute

paste-up dummy book or *layouts* with type matter from the *galley proof* cut up and pasted down to direct a) the artist as to the positioning and size of each illustration, and b) the printer as to the *make-up* of the book

perfect binding form of binding in which the back folds of the sections are cut off, roughened and covered with flexible glue instead of being sewn or stapled; a cheap form of binding used for many kinds of books, but particularly *paperbacks*; also known as thermoplastic binding

perfecting (1) printing or *backing-up* a sheet of which the other side has been printed; (2) printing a sheet on a *perfector*

perfector printing machine capable of printing both sides of a sheet in one operation using two impression cylinders

period (U.S.) full stop or full *point*

photo-engraving the process of producing *halftones* for *letterpress* or *offset lithography* by photographing the image through a screen to break up the tones into dots of equal density but varying size to make a halftone *block* or printing *plate*; *line artwork* is photographed without a screen

photographic composition (photo-setting) high speed typesetting on a machine using a photographic process instead of casting characters in *hot metal*, and producing as an end product either *film* or *bromides* from which *plates* can be made

photo gravure see *gravure*

photo-lithography see *lithography*, *offset lithography*

pica loosely a square of 12 *points* used as a unit of measurement; more correctly described as a pica *em*, of which six equal approximately one inch

pirated edition book printed without permission from the copyright owner

plagiarism the act of taking and using another person's writing, views, etc., as one's own

planographic printing any process in which the image-bearing areas are neither above nor below the surface of the printing plate, e.g. *lithography*, *collotype*; see also *printing processes*

plant (1) printer's machinery and equipment; (2) those items owned by a publisher which represent non-recurring expenditure, e.g. artwork, blocks, plates, film, etc.; recurring costs are those in which he will be involved when a book is reprinted, e.g. paper, binding materials, etc.

plate (1) metal printing surface fixed to a cylinder; (2) *stereo* for printing by *letterpress*; (3) illustration, normally printed on art paper

plate, lithographic of three kinds – a) surface plate, on which the image area is a light-hardened emulsion coating, giving good results up to 50,000 copies; b) deep-etched plate, on which the image is minutely below the surface and is reinforced with lacquer, to print up to 500,000 copies; c) bi-metallic plate, the most expensive, but capable of printing over a million copies

platen small *letterpress* machine in which the *chase* is upright; see also *press*

point printer's basic unit of measurement; 72 points = 0·9962 inch

point-size height of the type *body*, but not its width; see also *set*

portrait (of a book) upright in *format*

positive *film* made from a *negative*; it is *right-reading*

preface introductory matter to a book normally written by the author and appearing in the *preliminary pages*; sometimes acknowledgments are incorporated in it; see also *foreword*, *introduction*

preliminary pages (**prelims**) (U.S. front matter) introductory matter to the main text of a book, appearing in this order:
half-title
frontispiece
title-page
imprint (bibliographical details)
dedication
contents
list of illustrations
preface and acknowledgments
foreword
introduction

press (1) printing machine: -see opposite (2) printing establishment; (3) publishing organisation, particularly specialist or academic

press-cutting agency office which searches for and supplies to its subscribers *reviews* and other items about books published by them (U.S. clipping bureau)

print number (or **print run**) number of copies of a book to be printed – a crucial decision for a publisher, since on it will depend the *unit cost*

print out product of a computer which has been programmed; aspects of computer work particularly applicable to publishing are accounting, *sales analysis* and typesetting (see *computer typesetting*)

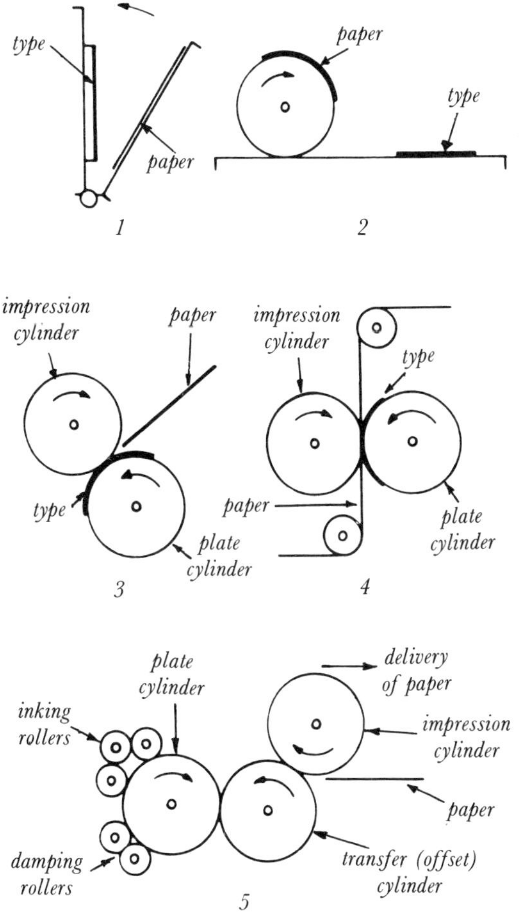

PRINCIPLES OF PRINTING PRESSES

(1) Platen press; (2) cylinder press; (3) rotary press (sheet fed); (4) rotary press (reel fed); (5) offset-lithography press

print to paper to use all the paper supplied for a particular job rather than work to a precise *print number*

printing processes the three main methods are – *offset lithography* on cylinder machines fed with single sheets or from a reel; *letterpress* on *flatbed* machines fed with single sheets or *rotary* machines using *stereos* or plastic plates and fed with single sheets or from a reel; *gravure* from flat copper plates or rotary from engraved cylinders and fed from a reel; see also *press*, *web-fed*

printing-off see *machining*

private press printing establishment normally printing and distributing in *limited editions* books of high typographical quality

privately printed not published for general sale, but for limited distribution, nevertheless still subject to *copyright deposit*

pro forma invoice *invoice* requiring payment for goods before delivery

process camera apparatus for photographing line, tone and colour subjects, *same size*, reduced or enlarged; see also *camera-ready copy*

process colours standardised colours yellow, cyan (blue) and magenta which, together with black, form the basis of four-colour printing (also known as full-colour printing)

process engraving photo-mechanical process for making printing blocks or plates

production ledger publisher's record of every item of expenditure on the production of a book as it is incurred; also of numbers printed, bound or in the form of sheet *stock* or *folded and collated*, etc., and their whereabouts

production and progress record complete record of each stage and of the progress of each item in the production of a book, e.g. paper purchase, *artwork*,

THE LETTERPRESS PROCESS

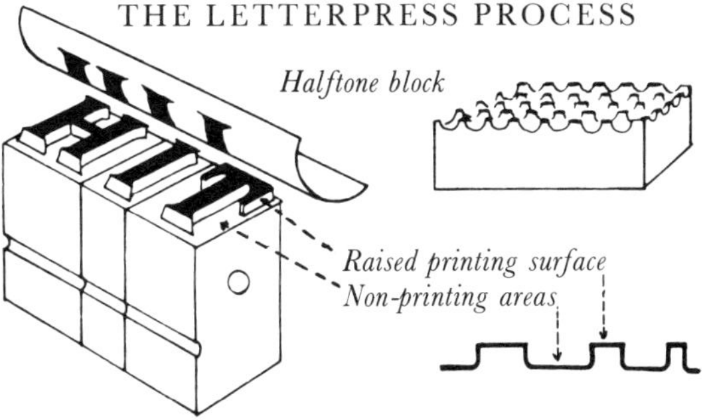

THE LITHOGRAPHIC PROCESS

Principle of the offset process

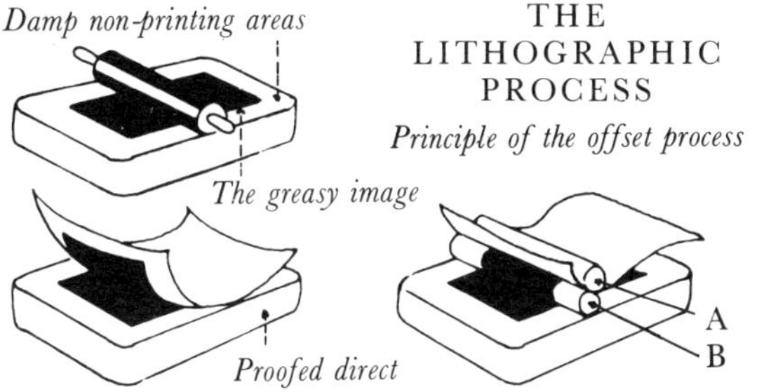

A *The rubber covered cylinder*
B *The impression cylinder*

THE GRAVURE PROCESS

The squares formed by the photogravure screen are all equal in size but vary in depth – and thus density, of ink.

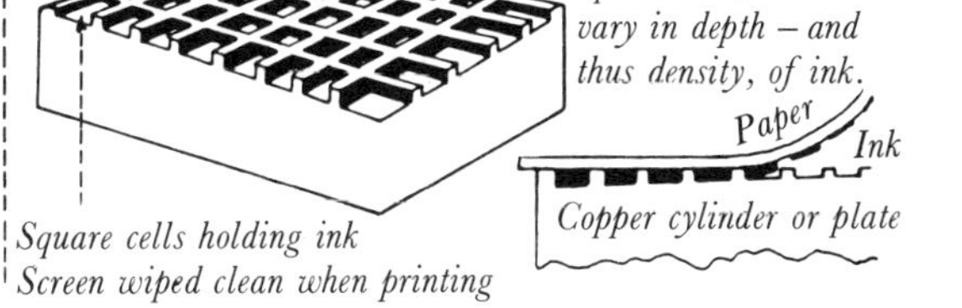

blockmaking, typesetting, *proofs*, delivery dates, etc.; essential for efficient working since a number of suppliers are likely to be involved

production schedule see *schedule, production*

profit and loss account comparison between revenue and expenditure over a year's trading; see also *accounting terms*

progressive proofs (**progressives**) *proofs*, from colour sets of *blocks* or plates, on which each colour is printed on its own and also progressively combined with the other colours, showing the quality of each colour and the effect of the colours when combined in printing

proof trial printing or reproduction of typeset matter or illustration:

AUTHOR'S PROOF usually proof on which the printer's reader has marked in green corrections and queries for the publisher

BLOCK PROOF (or block pull) proof of a design and illustration from a *letterpress block*

GALLEY PROOF first proof of typeset matter, on long strips of paper

MACHINE PROOF (or press proof) proof of *imposed* pages taken on the actual printing machine

OZALID (PROOF) photographic proof made from *film* before platemaking

PAGE PROOF proof in book form after *make-up* and *imposition*

PAGE-ON-GALLEY proof on long strips of paper of individual pages after *make-up* but before *imposition*

REVISED PROOF re-proofing of a particular stage with corrections incorporated (may be confined to those galleys or pages on which corrections have been made)

SLIP PROOFS (or slip pages) proof after *make-up* but before *imposition*, each page being on a separate piece of paper

proof copy *page proof* of a book, usually in a paper cover, particularly for advance circulation

proof correction checking a *proof* for errors made in *composition* and *make-up* and marking corrections; see pp. 52-3

proof reader one who checks a proof and marks corrections on it

provision accounting term for a reserve against a possible loss on a specific *title* or project, or an allowance for the loss before it is incurred

published price see *list price*

publisher person or company or institution legally responsible for issuing a particular book, and for the capital cost and financial risk involved in its publication, including the payment of *royalties* and/or fees; also used to describe that individual who is responsible for the administration of a *publishing house* or a division of it (in a small organisation the publisher is usually the principal – in a larger organisation he may be responsible for the viability of one area only); publishing functions include – selecting manuscripts for publication; commissioning authors to write books; negotiating and acquiring publishing *rights*; *editing* and *sub-editing* manuscripts for publication; *designing* the books; commissioning *artwork*; having type set; buying paper and other materials; having the books printed and bound; promoting the books; distributing copies to booksellers and suppliers; negotiating on the author's behalf the sale of *rights*

publisher's representative normally one who sells to and takes orders from *booksellers* and suppliers for the books of his employer; an educational representative, however, does not usually take orders in the U.K. from the schools and institutions he visits, but introduces books to them and acts as a link between the teachers and lecturers and his employer

Marginal mark	Meaning	Corresponding mark in text
γ	Insert (or substitute) inferior figure or sign	⋏ (or encircle letters or signs to be altered)
⌒	Close-up – delete space between letters	⌒ Linking words or letters
#	Insert space	∧
eq.#	Make spacing equal	⌊ Between words
less#	Reduce space	⌊ Between words
trs.	Transpose	⊔⊓ Between letters or words, numbered when necessary
centre	Place in centre of line	Indicate position with ⌐ ¬
⌐	Move to the left	⌐
¬	Move to the right	¬
n.p.	Begin a new paragraph	[Before first word of new paragraph
run on	No fresh paragraph here	⌒ Between paragraphs
spell out	The abbreviation or figure to be spelt out in full	Encircle words or figures to be altered
⋏	(Caret mark.) Insert matter indicated in margin	⋏
‘γ ’γ	Insert single quotation marks	⋏ ⋏
“γ ”γ	Insert double quotation marks	⋏ ⋏

Some standard proof correction marks

Marginal mark	Meaning	Corresponding mark in text
δ/	Delete (take out)	Cross through
⌢δ⌣/	Delete and close-up	⌢ ⌣ Above and below letters to be taken out
stet	Leave as printed (when words have been crossed out by mistake)	. . . . Under letters or words to remain
caps	Change to capital letters	≡ Under letters or words to be altered
s.c.	Change to small capitals	= Under letters or words to be altered
caps + s.c.	Use capital letters for initial letters and small capitals for the rest of words	≡ Under initial and = under the rest of the words
l.c.	Change from capitals to lower case	Encircle letters to be altered
bold	Change to bold type	~~~ Under letters or words to be altered
ital.	Change to italics	— Under letters or words to be altered
rom.	Change to roman type	Encircle words to be altered
w.f.	(Wrong fount). Replace by letter of correct fount	Encircle letter to be altered
9	Invert type	Encircle letter to be altered
X	Replace by similar but undamaged character	Encircle letter to be altered
Y	Insert (or substitute) superior figure or sign	⋏ (Or encircle letters or signs to be altered)

publishing date, publication date date fixed by the publisher to prevent unfair competition, before which no copy of the book may be sold to the public or *reviewed*

publishing house publishing company, sometimes issuing books under more than one imprint

pull proof from *letterpress* type or *block*

pullout folded *tip-in* or *insert* in a book which, when opened out, makes three or four pages, also known as foldout, gatefold, throw-out

q.v. Latin quod vide = which see (used in cross-references)

quad (sheet) sheet of paper four times the size of the basic sheet, the dimensions of which are obtained by doubling each dimension of the standard size, e.g. quad *crown* = 30″ x 40″, quad *demy* = 35″ x 45″; see also *paper sizes*

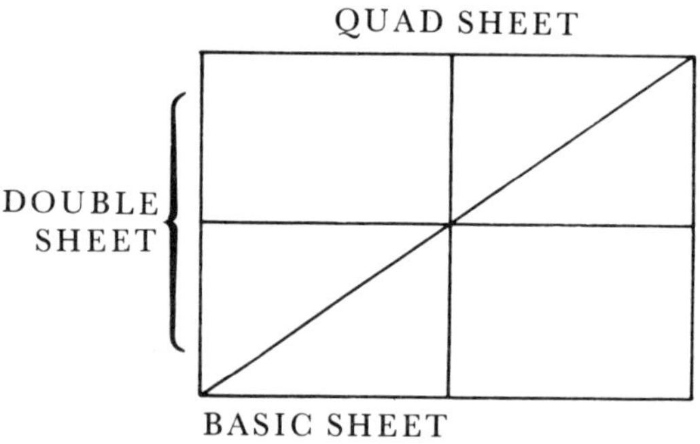

quarter-binding hard binding *case* of which the spine is covered with one material and the remainder in another, usually paper; see also *half-binding*, *full binding*

quarto (**4to**) size obtained by folding a sheet of paper twice, making eight pages

quire 25 sheets of paper; one-twentieth of a *ream*

quoted matter matter appearing in a book from a different source, normally set or arranged in a different style to distinguish it from the text

range to align lines of type; the instruction 'range left' (or, less often, 'range right') means that the lines referred to should be moved so that the beginning (or end) of each is aligned with the edge of the given type area; see *unjustified setting*

rare books see *antiquarian books*

reader (1) printer's *proof reader*; (2) one who reads manuscripts for a publisher and reports on their quality

reader's marks see *proof correction*

reading copy either a page *proof* or printed sheets of a book folded and bound in a paper cover and sent well in advance of publication to booksellers or librarians from whom a large order might be expected

ream originally twenty *quires* or 480 sheets; more often 500 sheets of paper of identical size, quality and make

recto right-hand page; see also *verso*

reel-fed (**press**) any *rotary* machine which prints on paper from a continuous reel, usually with attachments that will cut and fold the paper as part of the printing operation; also known as *web-fed*

register (1) (also noun) to align backing pages of type; or to position exactly blocks or plates in colour printing; (2) in bookbinding, a silk or cotton bookmark glued to the spine of the book

register mark mark (usually a cross) printed with each colour to ensure it is correctly superimposed, and trimmed off the sheet in the binding process

re-issue book, previously *out-of-print*, re-published in the same or a different *format* and treated as a new book for sales and publicity purposes

remainder book whose sales have dropped below an economic level and which is offered to booksellers and the public at a reduced price; normal *royalties* are not payable on remainders

representative see *publisher's representative*

reprint second or subsequent new *impression* or *edition* of a book, reprint *rights*, however, refer to editions of a book issued by another publisher, e.g. *paperback*, school edition, *book club*, etc.

repro(duction) pull careful printing by *letterpress* of illustration or text matter for photography and platemaking for printing by *lithography*; usually on art paper or high quality *antique*

residual rights *rights* which in the event of *reversion of copyright* to the author have not yet been leased by the publisher

retouch to alter an illustration or photograph to make it more suitable for reproduction, or to do this on the negative itself

returns books returned by a bookseller by agreement with the publisher

reverse left to right to turn an illustration so that the effect is that of seeing it in a mirror

reverse out (also **white out**) to transpose the normal relationship between image and non-image areas, particularly to enable type to appear as white out of a black or coloured background; the instruction to blockmaker is 'reverse black to white'

reverse reading reading from right to left, as for *letterpress* printing so that the type will appear on the paper the right way around; see also *right-reading*

reversion of copyright practice allowed for in most literary contracts whereby if after an agreed time the work goes *out-of-print* and the publisher is unwilling or unable to *reprint* it, all *rights* which have not yet been leased by the publisher revert to the author; see also *residual rights*

review copy finished copy of a book sent out to journals and other media for notice on or after *publication date*; see also *reading copy*

review list list of people, journals, etc. to receive copies of a book in advance of publication for the favour of a review

review slip small printed form inserted in a *review copy* of a book and giving information about title, price and *publication date*, before which no review shall appear

revise second or subsequent *proof* at a particular stage incorporating corrections

right-reading reading from left to right; *offset lithography* printing plates are right-reading

rights in a literary property these are of two main kinds –

(1) VOLUME RIGHTS (usually controlled by the publisher)

exclusive right, during the legal term of copyright or such other term agreed, to produce, publish and sell a work in book form in the original language throughout the territory determined between publisher and author

book club, cheap edition, paperback or other *reprint* rights leased to another publisher within the territory agreed upon

anthology quotation, digest and condensation rights, *one-shot* periodical or newspaper rights, strip cartoon rights, mechanical reproduction rights

(2) SUBSIDIARY RIGHTS (usually controlled by the publisher but sometimes by the author's *agent*) (U.S. neighbouring rights)

foreign rights (i.e. right to publish the work in a country outside the original territory)

translation rights
serial rights
film, broadcasting and television rights
advertising or other commercial use of the work or materials based on the work

rising space defect in letterpress printing whereby spacing material between two words rises to *type-height* and prints on the paper, showing up as a black rectangle

roman upright type as distinct from *bold* or *italic* (U.S. lightface)

rotary press printing machine on which the *plate* is fitted to the surface of a revolving cylinder; see also *press*

rotogravure *intaglio* printing on a *reel-fed* press

routing cutting into a *line block* to eliminate areas of unwanted matter

royalty payment, usually to an author, on the basis of a percentage of the *list price* of each copy sold or of the *net receipts* from sales

run see *print run*

running head *heading* at the top of a page, normally the title of the book on a left-hand page, the title of the chapter on a right-hand page; in dictionaries and encyclopaedias the title of the first and last entries on that page; also known as headline

running sheet printed sheet taken directly from the machine after printing has begun; if a fault is spotted, the machine can be stopped before too much paper is wasted; see also *machine proof*

run-on (1) to continue with new matter without a paragraph break; (2) to allow the printing machine to continue to run after an *edition* has been printed, with a view to using the sheets thus printed for a separate edition; such sheets, produced at 'run-on cost', can be budgeted at little more than the cost of paper and machine time

run-round to vary, at *composition* or *make-up* stage, the arrangement of type from the standard *measure* to allow for the insertion of an illustration

saddle-stitching binding by means of thread or wire through the fold; see also *side-sewing*

sale or return books supplied on the understanding that unsold copies may be returned after an agreed period and not paid for; see *consignment* and *see safe*

sales analysis analysis of sales usually according to type of book and sales area or region, as well as by *title*

sales plan outline of marketing policy for a book, including publicity, advertising etc.

same size (**s/s**) indication that artwork, etc. should be reproduced without reduction or enlargement

sanserif, sans-serif type designed without finishing strokes at the end of a line or bar of a letter or character; see also *grotesque*

scale to mark an illustration for reduction or enlargement as needed

schedule, editorial detailed, list, often on a preprinted card or sheet, of all stages in the preparation and production of a book in which *editorial* work is involved, with the date on which each must be completed in order to meet the production schedule; some such stages are delivery of manuscript, discussions with author about possible changes, *copy preparation*, permissions for use of copyright material, *proof* reading, illustration and cover design, index etc.; see also *schedule, production*

schedule, production detailed list, agreed with the printer, of all stages in the production of a book, with the date on which each must be completed if publication date is to be met and the printer be able to keep his price within his *estimate*; some such stages are manuscript for *cast-off* and *specimen page*, manuscript for *composition*, materials bought and supplied to the printer, illustrations and cover design for reproduction, *proofs* received and returned to printer, etc.; see also *schedule, editorial*

scoring process of creasing boards which form the binding of *paper-bound* books to prevent them breaking and to facilitate opening

scout one who, usually on a freelance basis, seeks out material for a particular publisher

screen fine grid of cross-hatched lines on glass or film placed between the original and the lens of a camera, dividing the image into dots which vary in size according to the tonal values picked up by the camera; the resulting *block* or printing *plate* will then give the impression of tones in correct correspondence with the original; common screen rulings vary between 55 and 150 lines per square inch (up to about 65 being normally referred to as 'coarse screen'), but the screen to be used depends on the paper and the printing process which will be employed; for *lithographic* plate-making the screens are finer than for *letterpress* printing, and some machines are able to print from a 300 screen; see also *halftone, contact screen*

screen angle angle at which the *screen* is placed to the horizontal for photography, usually 45°, in which position the lines are least conspicuous; where two or more screened colours are to be superimposed, the screens are placed at various angles to avoid obtrusive patterns

screen tint tone of any colour, which can be made to vary between 10% and 100%, and which in the photography of the original can be transferred to a plate for printing by *lithography*

see safe books supplied similarly to *sale or return* but which may not be returned without specific agreement, e.g. in exchange for other titles or as a gesture of goodwill

self-cover *limp* cover which is on the same paper as that on which the book is printed and part of one of its sheets

self-ends *endpapers* which are part of the first and last sections of a printed book

separation (1) procedure in *process* colour-work by which a full-colour original is divided into the four process colours yellow, cyan, magenta and black; (2) artist's drawing in black on a sheet of paper or *overlay* which represents a single colour of a two-, three- or four-colour design

serial rights right to publish extracts from a literary work in successive issues of a journal or newspaper; first serial rights are those which allow serialisation before publication of the work in book form

serif finishing stroke at the end of a line or bar of a letter or character; see also *sanserif*

set (of type) see *compose*

set (noun) distance across the *shank* of a *type*: it is not constant for each letter; a typeface of narrow set will give more characters to the line than one of wide set

set-off transfer of ink from one freshly printed sheet to another

shank that part of a metal *type* which raises the character to the right height for printing by *letter-press*

sheet stock supply of printed sheets of a book, usually held by the binder, awaiting the time when it is necessary to bind them up

sheet-fed (press) machine which prints single sheets at a time, as opposed to a *reel-fed* or *web-fed* press; see also *press*

show-through degree of opacity to which type printed on one side of a sheet can be seen from the other side; see also *strike-through*

side-sewing stitching the book through the sides

through the *back margin* with thread or staples; also known as side-stitching

signature complete printed sheet, folded; normally consists of either 16 or 32 pages; also a mark, usually a letter, which is sometimes printed at the bottom of the first page of each section of a book

sixteenmo (**16mo**) size obtained by making four right-angle folds in a sheet, producing 32 pages

slip case case made to hold a single or several volumes for protection, so designed that the spine or spines show

slip pages see *page-proof*

slug solid line of type cast in metal in a composing machine

small capitals series of roman capital letters which align with the *x-height*, A, B, C, D, etc.; not normally available in *sanserif* type designs

solid (**setting**) type set with no interlinear space or *leading*

spacing interlinear white space, or *letter spacing* between characters or words

specification (1) all the details about a book, e.g. length of text, *format*, number of pages, *royalties*, fees, etc., from which an accurate estimate or *costing* can be made; (2) instructions to a printer as to the *typography* and *format* of a book, often accompanied by a *layout*

specimen page usually a *double-spread* of type, set according to the publisher's instructions, for a final assessment before being used as the style for the book

spine back edge of a book; on hardcover books usually *blocked* with the author's name, title and publisher's name or *colophon*; on paperbacks printed with author's name, title, publisher's name or colophon, and *I.S.B.N.*

spine lettering words on the back edge of a book;

usually running from top to bottom so that they can more easily be read when the book is lying flat

spoilage unavoidable wastage of materials, especially paper, during printing, folding and binding, which must be allowed for when materials are bought

spotting painting out unwanted spots or scratches on *negative film* before platemaking; also on photographs and artwork etc.; see also *retouching*

standing type/plates *letterpress* type or *lithographic* plates stored in readiness for further printing; see also *keep standing*

stereo (type) duplicate of type and/or *blocks* cast in metal from a papier-mâché or plastic mould and then brought to *type-height* for printing

stet Latin = 'let it stand', denoting that a correction should be cancelled

stock unsold copies of books or materials

stock paper sizes sizes of paper which are normally held by a paper merchant or paper-mill for immediate delivery

stock valuation estimate of the value of a publisher's stock of books; in an annual balance sheet this stock is shown as an asset, but publishers usually 'write down' periodically to net realisable value or below title by title so as to present a realistic picture of the company's finances; such estimates are normally subject to an auditor's agreement

straw-board stiff material for *case* binding made from pulped straw

strike-through penetration of ink through the paper

strip-in combine different items of *film* before the plate-making process

sub-edit (of a book) to check the details of a typescript for language, style and usage, and to ensure that it conforms to *house style*; to question matters of accuracy and fact; to ensure permissions have been obtained; to coordinate text, illustrations, cross-references, *captions*, *footnotes*, *index*, etc.; to read the *proofs*; and to present corrected and complete material to designer, compositor or printer at each stage in the book's production; see also *copy preparation*, *editorial work*, *proof reading*

sub-head heading subordinate to the main title of a chapter or article; particularly used in periodicals to break up long sections of text

subscribe (a book) secure orders for a book from booksellers before publication date

subsidiary rights see *rights*

subscription see *subscribe*

supercalendered paper paper given an extra smooth finish when passed through heated steel rollers (calenders) of a paper-making machine; see also *calendered*

superior figures raised figures in text to identify footnotes or other notes, i.e. ^{1}; inferior figures line up with the bottom of the descender, i.e. $_{1}$

tabular setting setting of figures (e.g. for statistical information) in columns

tail bottom edge of a book or folded sheet

tail-piece decoration or illustration at the end of a chapter

take back to move lines of text matter from a page to the preceding page, or a word or words from a line to the preceding line

tape (1) strip of strong woven material fixed across the back edge of a set of folded sheets of a book and pasted or glued to each side of the binding case to give it support; (2) roll of punched paper or magnetic tape from which type can be set on photocomposing machines or *hot-metal* typecasting machines

tensile strength durability of paper tested by the weight needed to break it

terms agreed basis of business between publisher and bookseller or supplier, covering length of credit, varying *discounts* for different types of book and for different quantities, etc.

text illustrations pictures printed on text pages and not supplied in the book as separate *plates*, *wraps*, *inserts*, etc.

thermoplastic binding see *perfect binding*

throw-out see *pullout*

tint see *mechanical tint*, *screen tint*

tip-in to paste a single leaf, e.g. illustration *plate* or *cancel*, into a bound book

title (1) name of a book, or part or chapter of a book; (2) separate publication on a publisher's *list*

titling capital type letters for which no *lower case* characters have been designed; as these have no descenders, the characters are larger than the normal type of the same *point* size

tool impress designs on to the binding of a book by means of heated tools, normally on single-copy leather-bound books

trade counter central place, separate from his warehouse, where *stock* is held by a publisher from which small orders from booksellers can be supplied

trade terms see *terms*

trading account see *profit and loss account*

trichromatic inks yellow, cyan and magenta inks used in *halftone* colour printing to achieve other colours by combination and by correct *etching* of blocks or plates; such inks are standardised for different printing processes

trim cut away edge or edges of a sheet of paper or of a page to reduce it to the required size; the top, bottom and outside edges of a book are trimmed to remove the folds so that the pages are separated; see also *binder's trim*

turnover total sums received during a given period from the sales of books and *rights* (including sums invoiced)

twice-up description of an illustration which has been drawn double the size it will appear in the finished book; see also *half-up*

type (1) piece of metal which has on it a character in relief from which an impression can be obtained;

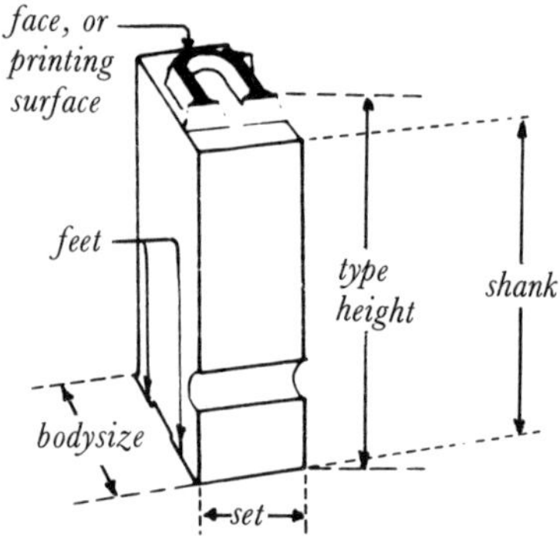

(2) collection of such pieces; see also *body*, *set*, *shank*

type area area of the page within which all text matter and illustrations are normally to be confined; usually identical for all pages in a given book

type rule ruler for measuring type, usually showing scales for 12 *point*, 6 point, 10 point, 5 point, 8 point

typeface particular design of type, known by a name and/or number; a type family may contain a number of typefaces

type-height standard height of metal type and blocks mounted for printing by *letterpress*, in U.K.

·0·918 inches (23·317mm); also called height-to-paper

typography craft of arranging type matter in an effective manner, requiring technical knowledge and artistic judgement

underline see *caption*

uniform edition set of books in an identical design

unit cost total *direct cost* of producing a book (including royalty advances) divided by the number of copies printed at one time; the selling price of the book is based on the unit cost

Universal Copyright Convention see *copyright*

unjustified setting type matter which is not set in lines of equal length; normally a maximum *measure* is specified, which the end of the line should approach as near as possible, but not exceed

upper case see *case*

varnish protective shiny surface applied to book covers or jackets by machinery or overprinting; not as thick, glossy or expensive as *lamination*

vehicle oily substance mixed with pigment of printing inks

verso reverse or back of a leaf forming a left-hand page; see also *recto*

volume one of a set of books, normally numbered consecutively, e.g. of an encyclopaedia

volume rights see *rights*

w.f. wrong *fount*; indication that a letter used in a line of type is of different design or *weight*

watermark design appearing in paper, made by a wiremark or by the impression of the *dandy roll* on the wet pulp on the papermaking machine

web wire mesh of a papermaking machine carrying the wet pulp

web-fed see *reel-fed*

web-offset printing from a reel of paper on a *rotary lithographic* press with a single or multiple units, particularly used for newspapers; for book printing, the printed reel of paper can be slit and folded by attachments to the machine, which can achieve an output of up to 22,000 sections per hour; see also *offset lithography*, *press*

weight (1) paper substance may still be measured in pounds per ream, but generally practice tends towards expressing it as grammes per square metre of a single sheet = gsm or g/m^2; (2) also refers to type (*bold*, light etc.)

weight conversion some metric measurements:

1 gramme (g) = 0·03526 oz
1 kilogramme (kg) = 2·205 lb
1 tonne (t) = 0·984 ton

U.S. UNITS

1 U.S. cwt = 100 lb
1 U.S. ton = 2000 lb
1 U.S. ton = 20 U.S. cwt

IMPERIAL OR BRITISH WEIGHTS

1 ounce (oz) = 28·350 g
1 pound (lb) = 16 oz = 454 g
1 stone = 14 lb = 6·350 kg
1 hundredweight (cwt) = 8 stone = 112 lb = 50·802 kg
1 ton = 20 cwt = 2240 lb = 1·016 t

white out see *reverse out*

wholesaler person or organisation buying books in bulk from publishers for resale to retail booksellers or libraries (U.S. jobber)

widow short, last line of a paragraph appearing as the first line of a page; regarded as bad typographical practice, and can be avoided by *overrunning* or *taking back* at *make-up* stage

wire stitching binding by means of wire staples rather than thread, a much cheaper process; see also *side-sewing*

woodcut relief-printing block of wood, produced by cutting along the soft grain; a wood engraving is cut across the grain; the ideal material is boxwood or some other hard wood

woodfree paper free of mechanical wood pulp, but using chemical wood (U.S. freesheet)

woodpulp paper pulp made from wood, largely by mechanical means; also known as *mechanical wood* (U.S. groundwood)

word division the use of a hyphen connects a broken word at the end of a line; such breaks are established by usage, often according to their phonetic syllables; some computer-assisted typesetting systems are capable of an automatic hyphenation routine

work-and-turn method by which, say, an 8-page oddment at the end of a book comprising sections of 16 pages may be printed as 8 pages to view on the same size of sheet, which is then turned and *perfected*; this enables the oddment to be printed on the same machine as the rest of the book, ensuring even inking and impression, while at the same time its *print run* is half the number of that for the other sheets

work-in-progress all items required for the production of as yet unpublished *titles* which have been paid for

wove paper *antique* paper made on a machine whose *screen* is a finely-woven wire mesh, thus avoiding the appearance of *laid* lines

wrap section of at least four pages wrapped round a *signature* and bound into the book with it; see also *insert*, *inset*

wrapper see *jacket*

x-height height of those characters in a *fount* of type which have neither ascenders nor descenders

Xerography proprietary process for copying by means of a dry photographic method

zinco line block for letterpress printing and for stamping ink on to the binding case of a book

SHORT BIBLIOGRAPHY

Blond, Anthony THE PUBLISHING GAME *Cape*, 1971

Butcher, Judith COPY-EDITING *Cambridge University Press*, 1975

Escarpit, Robert THE BOOK REVOLUTION *Harrap*, 1966

Glaister, Geoffrey A. GLOSSARY OF THE BOOK *Allen and Unwin*, 1960

Hart, Horace RULES FOR COMPOSITORS AND READERS *Oxford University Press*, 37th edition 1967

Jennett, Sean THE MAKING OF BOOKS *Faber*, 5th edition 1973

Landau, Thomas ENCYCLOPAEDIA OF LIBRARIANSHIP *Bowes and Bowes*, 1958

Martin, Robert E. A GLOSSARY OF BOOK TRADE TERMINOLOGY *Book Development Council*, 3rd edition 1973

Mumby, F.A. *and* Norrie, Ian PUBLISHING AND BOOKSELLING *Cape*, 5th edition 1974

Plant, Marjorie THE ENGLISH BOOK TRADE *Allen and Unwin*, 3rd edition 1974

Unwin, Sir Stanley THE TRUTH ABOUT PUBLISHING *Allen and Unwin*, 7th edition 1960

Williamson, Hugh METHODS OF BOOK DESIGN *Oxford University Press*, 2nd edition 1966